Discover

Turtles & Tortoises

by Victoria Marcos

© 2018 by Victoria Macos
ISBN: 978-1-53240-539-6
eISBN: 978-1-53240-540-2
Images licensed from Fotolia.com
All rights reserved.
No portion of this book may be reproduced
without express permission of the publisher.
First Edition
Published in the United States by
Xist Publishing
www.xistpublishing.com
PO Box 61593 Irvine, CA 92602

The terms "turtle" and "tortoise" are used interchangeably depending on where you live in the world. Turtles have been around for more than 200 million years. They live in warm and mild waters and climates on every continent except for Antarctica. Turtles can live up to 150 years.

Turtles range in size from the smallest speckled tortoise which is less than 4 inches long to the largest

leatherback sea turtle which weighs 1,500 pounds. There are about 300 species of turtles living today.

The turtle's domed shell is called the "carapace" and the flat underside is called the "plastron." The shell is made up of 60 different bones connected together. The shell is covered with skin-like plates called "scutes."

All turtles breathe air. Sea turtles spend almost all their time underwater. When they surface for a breath, they exhale and inhale quickly, then dive back under.

9

Sea turtles mostly eat seaweed, crabs, jellyfish, shrimp, snails, sponges, algae, and mollusks.

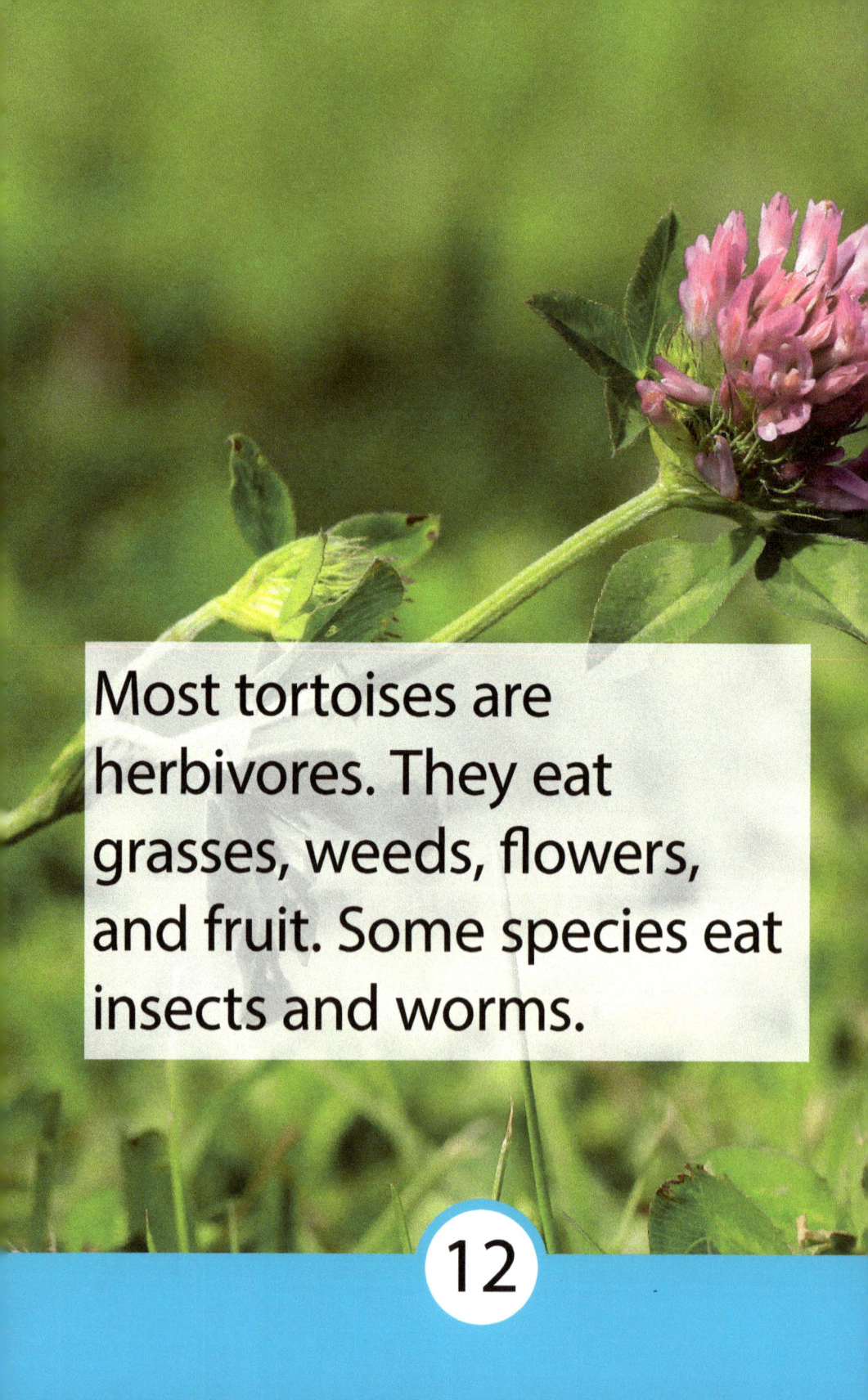

Most tortoises are herbivores. They eat grasses, weeds, flowers, and fruit. Some species eat insects and worms.

13

14

Turtles begin to vocalize while still in their egg. They communicate to each other about when to hatch and make their way out of the nest. Mothers will make sounds to guide their babies to the correct path of migration.

Most turtles can retract their head and legs into their body.

This is a very good defense against predators.

17

Unlike tortoises that have claws and sea turtles that have flippers, semi-aquatic turtles have webbed feet that help them swim better.

Just like you can tell the age of a tree by the number of its rings in its trunk, you can also sometimes tell the age of a turtle by the rings on its shell.

All turtles lay eggs. The pregnant female will dig a nest with her flippers when it's time for her to lay eggs. Some sea turtles swim as far as 1,400 miles to reach their nesting ground.

The mother covers the eggs in sand and returns to the sea. She will swim back to her feeding grounds until it is time for her to nest again in two to three years. Tortoises use their claws to dig burrows that can be up to 30 feet long.

The pregnant sea turtle will return to the same nesting ground she was born in to lay 50-200 eggs, depending on the species. After 50-60 days, it's time for the eggs to hatch. Baby turtles use their "egg-tooth" to break out of their egg's shell and dig through the sand and out of their nest.

Once they are out, they are able to survive on their own. Baby sea turtles instinctively go into the sea shortly after birth.

Since they are cold-blooded and take on the temperature of their environment, turtles are hot when it's hot and cold when it's cold.

To help control their temperature, they build south-facing burrows to stay warm and north-facing burrows to stay cool.

Giant tortoises are some of the largest tortoises in the world. The oldest giant tortoise in captivity is thought to be over 250 years old.

www.ingramcontent.com/pod-product-compliance
Lightning Source LLC
LaVergne TN
LVHW010317070426
835507LV00026B/3439